The Night Sky

by Vaishali Batra

OXFORD
UNIVERSITY PRESS
AUSTRALIA & NEW ZEALAND

Look Up!

Have you ever looked up at the sky at night?

There's a lot to see!

Let's take a closer look at the Moon, stars and planets!

Our Moon

Our Moon is a giant body of rock.

It has lots of **craters** on its grey surface.

crater

light

Light from the Sun **reflects** off the Moon.
This is what makes the Moon glow.

The Moon in Orbit

The moon **orbits** our planet. Each orbit takes just over 27 days.

The sun lights up different parts of the moon as it orbits our planet. This makes it look like the moon is changing shape.

full moon

new moon

Stars

Stars look tiny to us as they are so far away, but they are huge!

Stars are made of very hot chemical **gases**.

Some stars explode! This is called a supernova.

The blast is very bright.

The North Star

The North Star is an important star in the sky.

It is very bright and stays in almost the same spot.

North Star

People have used the North Star for thousands of years to help them **navigate**.

The North Star showed sailors which way to go.

The Sun

Our Sun is actually a star. It is by far the closest star to our planet ... but it's still millions of miles away!

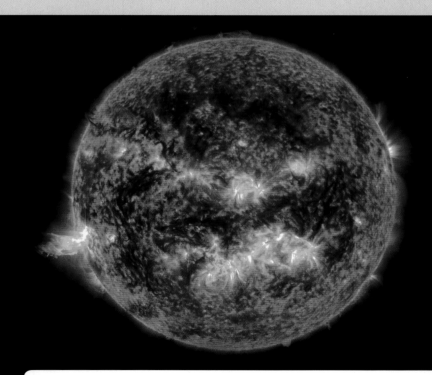

The Sun is 4.5 billion years old!

Life would not exist on our planet without the Sun.

It gives us light, heat and energy.

Our Solar System

This is our solar system! All the planets orbit the Sun.

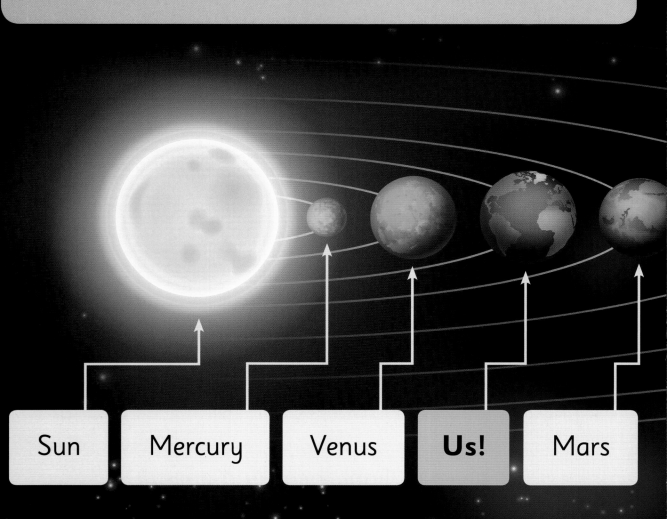

| Sun | Mercury | Venus | **Us!** | Mars |

Not to scale

There are eight planets in our solar system. Each planet moves around our sun in the same direction.

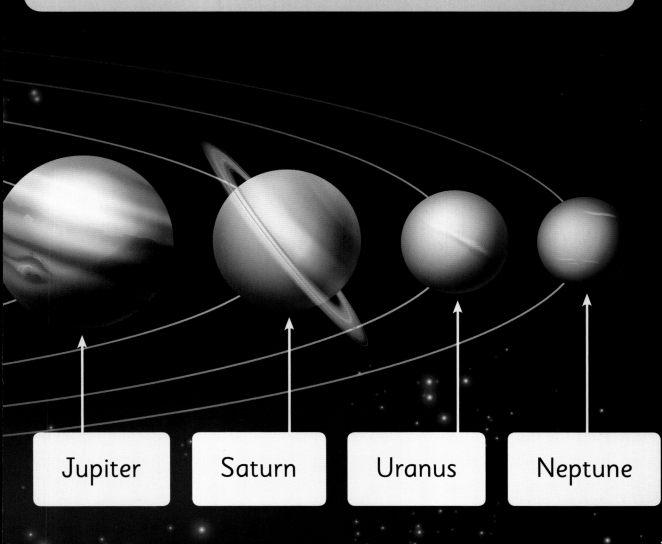

Jupiter   Saturn   Uranus   Neptune

The Planets

Mercury is closest to the Sun.

Venus is the hottest planet.

Mars looks red!

Jupiter is the biggest planet.

Saturn has icy rings.

Uranus looks blue!

Neptune is cold and windy.

Galaxies

A galaxy is made up of dust, gas and billions of stars.

Our solar system is part of a massive galaxy called the Milky Way Galaxy.

Our solar system

The Milky Way

Technology

Technology has helped us find out about space.

This is the Hubble Space Telescope.

These are some amazing photos that the Hubble Space Telescope has taken.

Keep Looking!

Keep looking up at the night sky. There are amazing things to see!

Glossary

craters: large holes made by objects hitting the ground

gases: substances like air that are not solid or liquid

navigate: to plan how to get to a place

orbits: travels around a planet, star or moon

reflects: when light bounces off a surface

Index